T0209326

Within My Illusions invites us to pause and reflect on the wondrous inner world of sensation, image, emotion, and thought. The heart of what this treasure reminds us is the magnificent experience of being alive, here, in this precious unfolding we call our life. Each entry illuminates the subtle majesty of the present moment, the meaning of inner reflections and interactions with people, pets, and the planet, the ways our past preoccupations and anticipations of the future inevitably shape our perceptions—our "illusions"—in constructing our experience of now. Taken together, there is a magical synergy that binds these powerful poems, bridging image and idea, the profound and the mundane, in ways that linger still, inspiring this mind, long after the pages of this wondrous book have been closed, to open in new and grateful ways beyond what words can say.

Daniel J. Siegel, M.D.
New York Times Bestselling Author of *Mind*, *Aware*, and *Brainstorm*;
Executive Director, Mindsight Institute
Clinical Professor, UCLA School of Medicine

When you enter Jennifer Bloom's work, you enter Jennifer Bloom's heart. Walk with her on this trail of truths and illusions. As Jennifer remembers herself as a Miracle, you might remember that you, too, are a Miracle. You might remember the way miraculous Love can squeeze through the narrowest cracks to fill the Primal Soul. You might remember that Love has been inside you all along, and that Love breaks the shackles that bind and shows you the way to freedom.

Pamela Eakins, *Tarot of the Spirit*

Within My Illusions is a coffer, each poem a gem. With poignant, vivid detail, Bloom invites the reader to explore our habits, our patterns of thought, and our belief systems in a quest for spiritual awakening. Timely and wise, Bloom's second volume of poetry nourishes in the moment and long after the last page has turned.

Jennifer Hritz, author of *Smoke and Glass* and *The Crossing*

With heart, soul, wit, and a presence you can feel as you read her words, Jennifer Bloom's poetry is the spark of inspiration, hug from an understanding friend, and hope for a new world we can all use during times of change and uncertainty. Get this book for yourself, give it to friends, and use it in the gatherings you facilitate to open the hearts and minds of those you love and influence.

Christine Arylo, MBA, women's leadership advisor
and best-selling author, and founder of The Feminine Wisdom Way

Also by Jennifer Bloom

Brainstorms (poems)
The Only Way out Is Through (songs)

Poems

WITHIN

By

MY

Jennifer

ILLUSIONS

Bloom

BALBOA.PRESS

A DIVISION OF HAY HOUSE

Balboa Press books may be ordered through booksellers or by contacting:

Balboa Press
A Division of Hay House
1663 Liberty Drive
Bloomington, IN 47403
www.balboapress.com
844-682-1282

Because of the dynamic nature of the Internet, any web addresses or links contained in this book may have changed since publication and may no longer be valid. The views expressed in this work are solely those of the author and do not necessarily reflect the views of the publisher, and the publisher hereby disclaims any responsibility for them.

The author of this book does not dispense medical advice or prescribe the use of any technique as a form of treatment for physical, emotional, or medical problems without the advice of a physician, either directly or indirectly. The intent of the author is only to offer information of a general nature to help you in your quest for emotional and spiritual well-being. In the event you use any of the information in this book for yourself, which is your constitutional right, the author and the publisher assume no responsibility for your actions.

Any people depicted in stock imagery provided by Getty Images are models, and such images are being used for illustrative purposes only.
Certain stock imagery © Getty Images.

Cover and Interior Image Credit: Sharon Zeugin
Cover Design Credit: Levi Slayer

Print information available on the last page.

ISBN: 978-1-9822-5194-9 (sc)
ISBN: 978-1-9822-5196-3 (hc)
ISBN: 978-1-9822-5195-6 (e)

Library of Congress Control Number: 2020913814

Balboa Press rev. date: 09/30/2020

Contents

Invitation ix

1. Discovery 1
   Miracle 3
   Security Blanket 4
   Sprouts 6
   Training Wheels 7
   Words I Love, in English 8
   Syllabus 10
   Trust 11
   Being the Way That I Am 12
   Work in Progress 14

2. Conversation 17
   Sunrise 19
   Eavesdropping 20
   Peaks and Valleys 22
   The Butterfly and the Gorilla 24
   The Tide Came in Faster Than I Expected 25
   I Only Said It Once 26
   The Trouble with Compassion .28
   Limits 30
   Separately Together 31
   The Path of a Butterfly 32

3. Impression 35
   Imprint 37
   Sometimes the Feelings Are So Big 38
   Longing 40

Tenderness 41
Each Moment a Snapshot 42
Spring Cleaning 44
Kaleidoscope. 45
On the Curious Paradox of Being Seen 46

4. Vessel 49

Two of Us 51
Freedom 52
fences 54
Odd Things Humans Do 56
In the Looking Glass. 58
How to Ask. 59
Some Days I Need to Choose to Not See the Mess 60
For My Friend in Rehab 62
How to Pack 63

5. Indescribable. 65

Lingering. 67
Sometimes I Dance. 68
They tried to contain her. 69
The Hummingbird and the Fly. 70
A Void That Contains Everything. 72
Mystery. 74
paradox 75
Dilemma. 76
Immersed 77
Gratitude Is Like a Giddy Toddler. 78
Truth Tears 80
Possibility 81

6. Illusions 83

The Net 85
A Poem about Spring 86
Rebel Flowers 87

The Trail Is Just a Suggestion 88
Falling Apart. 90
The Landscape Is Always Changing .92
Parental Controls 93
Find the Joy Anyway. 96
Primal Heart. 98
Letting Go 100
The Story Is Not Who I Am. 101

Acknowledgments. 103

About the Author. 107

Invitation

Let this book of poetry present itself as an invitation. You can read the poems in any order or straight through. You may want to linger on one poem at a time or take in the book all at once. You may choose to read the poems as an observer, a witness to my heart and experience. Or, I invite you to bring your own heart to the conversation. Hold the book in your hands, close your eyes, and in your imagination feel the space of your heart. In the stillness or movement of your imagination, notice what emerges from that heart space—it could be an image, a question, or a thought. Open the book and see where your eyes land. Read that poem out loud, in your own voice to feel its resonance. How does your heart connect with that poem?

You might take a few moments to pause and reflect or even write down some thoughts in a journal. I'm always in awe at the way, when we open to connect, we become mirrors, experiencing ourselves in an expanded way through one another.

I offer these poems as one side of a conversation. I invite you, the reader, to join me.

- 1 -

DISCOVERY

Let's be as children,
Eager to discover things
We already knew.

Miracle

Her name tag said "Miracle,"
which seemed something lyrical.

I asked how she got her name,
though I could imagine the story
even before she told it.

I just wanted to see the way her face lit up
as she remembered
who she was.

Security Blanket

When I was born,
my grandfather gave me a blanket,
soft flannel, quilted in satin,
the color and feel of a pale, pink rose.
Stitching in the center outlined the shape of a teddy bear.
The border was edged in creamy white.

When I could speak,
I named the blanket Mercy.
I was three.
How could I know what mercy was,
or the ways in which I would need it?

Mercy would be my cocoon,
my womb, when the world inside me felt too big
and my strength to withstand it too small.

I rested Mercy against my cheek,
let her gentle presence sink into my heart.
I rubbed her edges between my fingers,
like a meditation.
Her cloth graced my lips,
a prayer,
a relief
from feelings I didn't know how to speak.

I slept with Mercy every night,
and the space she held for me expanded
even as she grew smaller,
receding with time,
like the tree in the story
I often read with her,

until one day she was mistakenly sent to a hotel laundry
with the rest of the bed linens.
I was fourteen.
I sobbed as I heard
the resignation in my dad's voice
as he spoke to the housekeeping department,
asked them if they could

Please. Look. One. More. Time

for a blanket,
once pink,
now beige,
edges frayed,
torn and laced
in spots where fingers
had worn through,
where mercy reigned.

Sprouts

Underneath the heavy weight of fear,
The shoulds, the coulds,
A path that seems unclear;

Beneath the snow-white winter of my mind,
Where flowers droop and
Petals wilt in space confined;

A steady chant has quietly begun:
Feed me.
Water me.
Point me in the direction of the sun.

Training Wheels

My dad held onto the back of the seat
the first time I rode my bike
without training wheels.

"Don't let go," I pleaded.

I wasn't aware of when the bike
slipped out of his grip,
but I can still feel the moment
of bringing myself into balance,
of releasing my breath,
and finding the freedom to fly.

Words I Love, in English
(written three times and used in a sentence)

frisky
frisky
frisky
Snowball is frisky after a bath and hops around the deck like a kangaroo.

tickled
tickled
tickled
I was tickled by the boy saying, "When I have a basketball in my hand, I feel joy." He doesn't remember saying it, but I was paying attention.

basal ganglia
basal ganglia
basal ganglia
The basal ganglia is the part of the brain that controls routine and habitual behavior and thought processes; it's like autopilot; in my imagination, it's purple and has tentacles.

linger
linger
linger
I tend to linger until the last person goes, unless I leave early.

boisterous
boisterous
boisterous
I learned how to be boisterous from my sister, who is the funniest person I know; also from doing theater; it's not encoded in my basal ganglia; it requires focused attention, which involves a different part of my brain.

delightful
delightful
delightful
Most of my best friends have told me that when they first met me, they thought I was a bitch; but once they got to know me, they realized I'm delightful.

actually
actually
actually
Actually, I'm naturally reserved in new situations. This can come across as aloofness; and sometimes I just don't have anything to say, so I listen; and sometimes I'm overwhelmed or sad, or tired from being boisterous or just living; and sometimes I really want to go home and soak in a bath, which leaves me feeling tranquil and not frisky.

tranquil
tranquil
tranquil
The river appears tranquil on the surface, but deep down the current is raging.

Syllabus

I don't remember signing up for this class
or even seeing the syllabus.

If I had looked at the lesson plan,
the list of assignments,
the sequence of tests and quizzes,

I'm sure I would have passed it up
in favor of something more like
Compartmentalization 101 or
Skimming in Oblivion.

I am a master procrastinator,
and as I stare in the face of pop quiz #48
I can find fifteen different ways to avoid,
distract, or otherwise evade this task.

But it keeps circling back in one form or another.

I can wish for blinders, tunnel vision,
or anything else that would limit my perception.

But when I look up and see
that grand old tree blowing in the breeze,
the exquisite movement of its leaves,
the owl gazing down upon me,

I think how glad I am to know it through these eyes.

Trust

"Do you trust in the flow of life?"
was the question on the table,

as if I would be able to provide
a straightforward answer,

as if a simple
Yes or No
would suffice,

as if it was easy
to shed years of conditioning
insisting I had to be the one
to make things happen
to go out and grab the bull by the head,
instead of letting life lead the dance,
delegating to the universe and taking a chance.

There are possibilities that I can't dream of,
the way the earth brings more shades of green
than any human mind could conceive of,

the way a pansy peaks out
from the shadow of winter,
the cardinal returns,
the canyon teems with life again,

and I didn't have to do a thing.

Being the Way That I Am

I was sitting on a bench by the river,
enjoying a quiet moment between tasks
and some time to myself.

I was practicing a new way of seeing,
relaxing my eyes until the ground appeared to pulse
like a heartbeat.

I was writing this poem in my head
when a man called out to me.
"Don't be so weary," he said.

"I'm not weary," I replied,
"Just thinking."

He was sitting on top of a picnic table,
looking out at the water
and also at me.

He was wearing a New York Mets cap, and I commented,
"I'm going to New York, and you're wearing a New York hat."

"You want my hat?" he asked.

"No," I said, "I'm going to New York,
and you're wearing a New York hat
and I just noticed that.
I wanted to say something about it."

He smiled a gold, toothy smile.
"My mom's from New York, but I've never been."
"It's a different place," I told him.

"My mom's from Brooklyn," he said.
"I'm going to see my sister. She lives in Brooklyn too."

But perhaps a different Brooklyn.

I looked beyond him to the street,
to where my car was parked
in front of a city office building
where I'd spent time in a meeting earlier.
"Enjoy the springtime," I said and headed
up the small hill toward the road.

"Hey, when are you leaving?" he called out to me.
"Right now," I said. "I'm going right now."
"Have a good flight."

I started to walk away when
I had the urge to turn back and say,
"Thank you for talking to me."

"You're welcome," he said with a wave,
and then turned back to the river where my gaze followed
to take in the shape of this new friend,
sitting on top of a picnic table with his back to me,
looking out onto the water the way I often do,
appreciating the ebb and flow,
stillness and movement,
the gift of conversation,

and the thought,
"Perhaps I am weary."

Work in Progress

I am a work in progress,
Like the spiderweb outside my window
On the first day of fall.
The first day I noticed it
I thought it was perfect—
Intricate,
Delicate,
Concentric circles
Spanning two feet across,
A quintessential image.
An ephemeral thing
Strong enough to endure
Daily forces and pressures,
But easily forsaken
When a late afternoon thunderstorm
Rips through its fabric.

Yet the web is not abandoned.
The gaping hole
I saw the night before
Is filled by morning,
Sealed with a new weave,
Rendering it whole again.

I am a work in progress.
The unfinished painting,
The half-written poem,
The dough still rising.

I am the sky at dawn wondering
Why children are taught that I am blue
When right now I am pink-orange
And often the hue of deep space and filled with stars.

I am a work in progress.
Perhaps more like the spider than the web,
Mending tears
And tending to the cracks
That lace my heart.

I am a work in progress
And still I am
Complete.

2

CONVERSATION

Turning together,
A flock glides across the sea,
Enriched by its source.

Sunrise

My favorite way to watch the sun rise
is to look away and then back again.

Change often happens slowly,
imperceptibly,
as long as I'm staring straight at it.

I might miss the subtle shifts
from peach to blush to flame,
the way the heavy blanket of night
gently draws back,
allowing day to emerge again.

Eavesdropping

The old man sat
on the bench near mine,
beating the rhythm
of a slow waltz
as he tapped his cane on the dirt.
Rat tat-tat.
Rat   tat-tat.
Rat   tat-tat.

I wonder what it feels like
to live in his imagination.

I know myself in this way—
I need space inside my head
for thoughts to roam free,
to drift and soar
unbound by form,
a floating melody.

I've known it from the time I was born,
from the time I was a girl,
the times my mother would inquire,
"Penny for your thoughts?"

I sensed her disappointment every time I replied,
"Nothing."

But I couldn't break the spell.

Something magical was happening in that space,
something that wouldn't yet be contained by sentences,
identified by words or phrases,
or limited by periods.

And now I spend my days
threading words on a chain,
untangling strands of thought
and weaving them back together,
only to unravel the yarn
and knit a different pattern,
hoping that, over time,
fragments will approximate the whole.

Peaks and Valleys

A well-traveled peak will eventually become a plateau,
worn flat by footsteps and time.

The free-flying feeling of soaring down
a freshly paved hill on a bicycle,
unburdened by resistance,
is made possible by the effort it took to get up,
and will eventually lead
to another valley,
another hill to climb,
a new peak with its own unique
vantage point.

I might curse the hill on the way up.
I often do.
I can be tempted to turn around
or just shut down in a spot
that is neither here nor there,
all too aware of how far I am
from where I want to be.

At some point I might anticipate the feeling of joy—
no, awe—
when I reach the top,
heart pounding,
breath heavy,
endorphins flooding my body,
reveling in my strength and tenacity,
and the relief of being able to ride the momentum back down.

But the best part, the part I savor most,
is that moment when struggle lets go
and hope fades away,
and all that's left is me,
thumbs and forefingers gently cradling the gear shift,
and two wheels turning in perfect synchronicity.

The Butterfly and the Gorilla

The sorrow in his eyes is palpable,
she thought
as she stood in the palm of his hand,
locked in his gaze,
still as a stone,
light as a leaf.

Through her toes
she felt the slightest twitch
in fibers beneath calloused skin
and understood the effort it was taking to hold himself in place.

And she knew that she was not the one in danger.

The Tide Came in Faster Than I Expected

as I tried to navigate the space between the water
and the rocks that protected the shoreline.
Something primal kicked in
and I stretched my arm up
to save my phone,
still connected to my ears,
still drumming a steady beat.
Funny how instinct works.

I scrambled to the closest perch.
Salt burned the inside of my nose,
stung my eyes
as they blinked down
at the sea swirling beneath my feet,
where moments before I had stood on solid ground.
Too risky to wade around the rocks now.

I would have been bound to that place,
unsure of my balance, my strength, my agility,
trying to map out a path,
a trail that would guide me back to where I felt secure.
But the spray began to reach my ankles,
reminding me that I had no choice but to keep moving.

I Only Said It Once

but words jumped out of my mouth
like a reflex,
surprising me as much as they
surprised her.

It's not the sort of thing you say to a grandmother,
at least not to my grandmother,
at least not something I would say to mine.

No one else in the family regarded her
as the warm, nurturing type.
To me, she felt like a slice of the angel food cake she used to make,
soft and fluid as her collapsed soufflés,
gooey as the chocolate cookies we used to share.

I talked to her almost every day,
traveled to see her as often as I could,
and though I didn't always agree with what she'd say
and she didn't always agree with my choices,
we accepted each other.

In Chicago one day when I was twenty-two,
we walked down Michigan Avenue,
to visit her favorite jewelry stores—
just for fun—
and I tried on some pretty gems.

One store had a ring –
a band of gold coiled like a snake,
with a sparkly tail and ruby head.
I admired the way it slithered
up my middle finger.

Back out on the street
my grandmother and I agreed it was time for lunch
and started heading toward a restaurant.
"I'll get you the ring," she said,
"If you lose twenty pounds."

"Fuck you, Tia."

She got me the ring anyway.

The Trouble with Compassion

The trouble with Compassion is:
she steals from Anger,
who arrives with guns blazing
heart raging,
searching for a place to aim,
someone to take the blame.
Compassion robs Anger of its target,
sets it in slow orbit
to face off each opponent.

The trouble with Compassion
is the way she filters light,
reflects each being back to Anger
in such a way as if to say,
   "This one is doing the best he can."
     "This one, too, is doing the best she can."
       "Just like you are doing the best that you can."

Anger turns in measured circles, searching
for a place to land,
lurching this way and that, grasping at
the frayed end of a rope,
hoping to find something to take hold of,
until the only foe left is
Compassion herself.

But the trouble with Compassion is
her softness is formidable,
her lilac scent medicinal,
her truth too unequivocal,
and like a tender kiss
to a young child's head,

she gently nudges Anger's eyelids closed,
coaxing it into sweet repose
so it can settle down and drift
off to sleep.

Limits

I am standing
too close
to the fire.

I keep telling myself to take a step back,

but the warmth of your flame
won't
stop
drawing
me
in.

Separately Together

The butterfly flew across my windshield
the moment you said the word
"butterfly."

How could time regret what came before?
My day disjointed,
   your missed appointment,
      that moment I hesitated before walking out the door,

landed us here separately together,
converging in time if not in space.

you: soaking wet, stepping out of the spring,
   me: freshly coiffed, on the road, rambling,
      the swallowtail fluttering in between.

The Path of a Butterfly

"There are no straight lines in nature," he said,
One hand pressed against the stained oak cabinet,
His hip leaning on the polished granite counter.
"There are no flat surfaces; no right angles."

How could I not have noticed?

Now I look for them everywhere.
I look for lines in the way grass grows.
I search for angles in trees,
A smooth face of rock on which to rest.
But each blade of grass curves a little differently;
Each limb emerges in a peculiar way;
The ground pokes at my seat.

I see the path of a storm twist and turn up the jagged coastline,
Boundaries blur between colors of a rainbow.
Even my body is all curves,
Expanding and contracting with each breath
As I sit,
Pen in hand,
Searching for the linear narrative of this journey.

But life does not unfold in a straight line.
It spirals like the path of a butterfly.
It putters along quietly then opens wide,
Explodes in torrents,
Floods of action and emotion,
Leaving puddles and pools in its wake.

I am standing at the edge of the story.
In the reflection, I make meaning
From angles not right
Or wrong, but different;
Each lens offering its own perspective.
The story changes every time I tell it.

Words can only approximate
A narrative that spirals,
Weaving echoes from the past
As our tales twine together,
As we decide which will be the next step:
The one fueled by fear
Or the one guided by courage and compassion.

We are standing together at the edge of this story.
I will pass you my pen.
Together, we will write the next chapter.

3

IMPRESSION

Though words fade with time,
The impression of your hand
Remains on my heart.

Imprint

When I was a little girl
and I got hurt, my mother
tried to comfort me.

Held in her embrace,
tears veiled my face as I cried,
"I want to go home."

Over and over and over again:
"I want to go home."

"You are home," she would say.
"We are at home."

Over and over and over again:
"I want to go home."

Sometimes the Feelings Are So Big

Sometimes she's like a wild animal.
Screaming.
Writhing.
Thrashing.
A tangled mane of brown-black locks
Coiling down to her waist,
Plastered by tears to the sides of her face.
Fierce.
Contorted.
Eyes violent with rage.

One day I asked her if it's like the feelings are so big that her body can't
hold them.

"Yes."

There were times I hit myself so hard that I thought I might split in two.
Or maybe I hoped I would.
I imagined my skull cracked open,
Releasing a pressure accumulated
Over so much time,
Releasing the pieces of me
I had stuffed inside.

I hated the rage more than I hated the cause of the rage,
Or what I thought was its reason.
I hated myself for the feeling
That now I see reflected in this being,
This child I accept completely
In a way that I was unwilling to accept myself.

Her tempest passes quickly.
They always do.
And today she moves on to make a list
Of popsicle flavors for a pool party.
Clouds linger around me a bit longer,
Oscillating between grief and anger,
Two sides of the same coin.
Could it be the same with awe and despair?

Lying in bed,
Each of us spent,
Our foreheads rest gently together
As we say three things we are thankful for.
"Catharsis," I think, though I don't say it.
Tears stain my cheeks, as invisible as
The scars on my heart.

"I almost told you I was sorry for crying in front of you,
But I'm not sorry."

Sometimes the feelings are just so big
That my body can't hold them.

Longing

It pools
like molten wax.

A
flame
burns
through
the
very
thread
that
sustains
it,

moving slowly,
steadily
away
from its desire,

descending
deeper
into
the
cavity
of an open heart.

Tenderness

we sit not talking as a breeze wafts
the pages of my book, and wisps of hair
tickle my face when they escape the hold
of an elastic band. your hand stretches
to nestle them behind my ear.

it's not that we have run out of things to say
to one another. sometimes there's nothing
that needs to be said.

Each Moment a Snapshot

Light and shadow filter
through the reflections of my memory,

trying to recapture the details
of a little girl's laugh
from the way she reaches
with outstretched arms
to offer a handful of seashells,

zooming in on a sun-weathered table,
weary lines on the edges
of eyes that long to tell
a story.

If I could still
this life,
distill it down
to one frame,
would I be able to capture
the entirety of my existence?

Slowing down to inhale,
water warms on my wrists and hands,
soap accumulates,
caressing the insides of the crystal vase,
a gift, chipped on one side
of its hexagonal mouth.
My finger lingers there.
I held onto it despite
its imperfection.

Each moment a snapshot,
holding onto time,
even as it blurs around the edges,
even as the forms begin to fade.

Spring Cleaning

She held the dress close to her face
and breathed in
the memory.

Salty lips,
Savory kiss,
Sandalwood essence lingering in her hair.

And though she knew she would never wear it again,
She placed the dress in the "keep" pile.

Kaleidoscope

Could a tapestry woven over
forty-five years be reduced
to a single thread?

Mother and daughter
growing alongside one another,
crystals in a kaleidoscope
comprised of all mothers and daughters
across time.

With each turn,
the pattern changes,
pieces land in formations
simple and clear.
With another shift,
a new image
appears
fractured
then tumbles
into fresh coherency.

On the Curious Paradox of Being Seen

Contradiction
It's curious I feel
the simultaneous desire to be seen
and the fear of being
visible.

Impermanence
I am constantly changing.
Even now as you turn your gaze
and your eyes meet mine,
I will shift in ways both
imperceptible and
profound.

Complexity
I am as vast as the ocean,
as intricate as the shore.
I can spread my wings to envelope the Earth
and burrow into depths
you didn't even know
existed.

Judgment
You may admire too much
the charming iridescence of a seashell,
and forget that the other side is pointed and rough.
Or worse, you might be tempted
to regard one side as
superior.

Reflection
You can only see me though your self.

And in looking back at you, I must see my own likeness.
I thus become like the illusion
created by parallel mirrors,
receding into
infinity.

Truth
I will disappoint you.
We will disappoint each other.
So could we abandon expectations,
Let them fall by the wayside
like psychic road kill?
Who knows – we just might surprise one another.

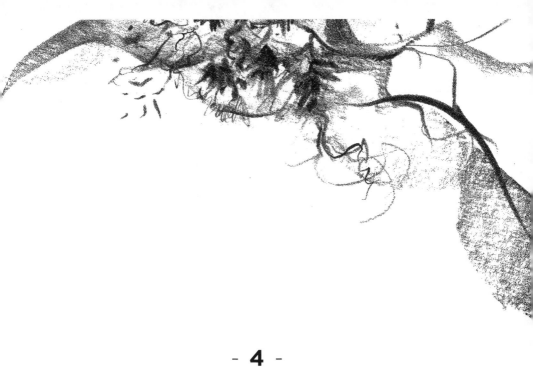

- 4 -

VESSEL

Her vessel expands
To hold space for its contents
And not the reverse.

Two of Us

The little girl inside me is the only thing moving.

I can't.

Both feet on the floor.
Grounding?
Right arm resting on glass tabletop.
Touching, but not feeling.
Sinking into a place
I don't recognize.
Anesthetized
by my own
grief.

"There are two of us in this body,"
is the thought that haunts me.
And if I can build a wall to protect her, I will
let myself believe that holding in
the outward expression of my feelings
means the feelings don't exist;
that I can keep her safe in her cocoon
by holing up in the fortress with her;
that shoring up the façade of a crumbling structure
is more valiant than allowing it to fall apart.

Freedom

I do not know what it feels like
to be trapped in my own skin,
confined
by a structure that doesn't seem to fit,
resigned to getting through one more day,
trying to make the best of it.

I wouldn't be able to describe the sensation
of trying to smother a rage
that burns so deeply
it feels like I am waging a war upon myself,
suffocating flames of a fire
until what's left inside
is only the hopeless smoldering
of an unfulfilled dream.

I couldn't tell you what it's like
to be silenced or shamed,
bullied or blamed,
discarded, disregarded,
ignored, deplored,
minimized, despised
just for being
alive.

But I can stand at the edge
of the earth
and the sea
and the sky,
watching the feathered creatures fly
as the sun takes its evening dive,
and imagine what it feels like
to be free.

fences

it was always meant to be temporary.
intended to be removed and replaced
by something with more substance.

the pliant green wire was barely strong enough
to support the weight of the canyon.
vines crept up and over
until the fence bowed in places
that would make a good entry point
for something larger than I would choose
to invite in.

there were times when Snowball disappeared
for just a few minutes longer than usual,
and I couldn't help but wonder if the time had come
when she'd discovered that the limits of the boundary
were only in her mind.

the new fence is just what I asked for.

and yet,
there is that part of me.

the part that longs to go back
to the one day
when there was no divide,

the day when all I could see
was a faint impression of the old fence,
the new one still in pieces on the ground.

the day I stood in the middle,
savoring the limbo between old and new.

the day I walked to the edge of an artificial border,
feeling for a moment
that there was no separation
between the pebbled ground where I stood
and the wilderness that surrounded me.

Odd Things Humans Do

(as described by a human who does odd things)

Put objects in boxes
With labels
On high shelves
In closets
And pretend
That if they can't see them, they don't exist.

Build fences around backyards
Then plant rosebushes in the front
And complain when the deer eat the flowers.

Spend time.
Waste space.
Plan.

Stifle sneezes.
Suppress laughter.
Smother smiles.

Struggle.
Resist.
Refuse to let go.

Compare themselves to others.
Compare themselves to anything.
Compare anything to anything.

Tell each other what to do,
Or how to feel,
Or whom to love.

Make rules about love.
Put limits on love.
Look in the mirror and see anything other than love.

In the Looking Glass

I wish that you knew
How important you are,
Your pure-hearted presence
And soft-spoken truth.

I wish you understood
That your strength
Lies not in pushing against,
But in that subtle grace
That moves you through each day,
The surprisingly wise things you say
When you think you are saying
Nothing.

I wish I could hand you a mirror,
And in that reflection
You'd see perfection.

I wish that you could see yourself
Through my eyes.

How to Ask

Snowball knows
how to ask for what she desires.

She jumps on the sofa,
squirms around in circles,
creates as much of a ruckus as she can,
then lands on her back,
paws in the air,
neck lifted
tilting her head
up and back
in my direction.

Moments later,
in an elaborate commotion,
she flops herself over like a fish
on dry land.
A new position:
belly up
spread-eagle
head turned to the side,
eyes pleading,
"Don't you see me?

Eventually.
Inevitably.
I will stop what I am doing,
settle in next to her for a snuggle.
Close my eyes—
and smile.

Some Days I Need to Choose to Not See the Mess

There's a giant inflatable orca in my entry hall.
I've kicked him closer to the front door
To clear a path from my daughter's room to mine
So she won't trip when she makes her 2 a.m. visit.
Now it looks like he's standing guard.

A pile of cheap, made-in-China toys
Hatched from pastel plastic eggshells,
Dumped next to a pink basket.

Flowers once vibrant
Begin to wilt.

Earbuds wires,
Charger wires,
Phones, Pads, and Books
Tethered to walls.
Remote control batteries
Abandoned on countertops
Instead of in the recycling box.
I really should buy the rechargeable kind.

Stacks of washed containers
Piled high on the right side of the sink,
The left side blissfully empty.

Paper and books and journals
Piled in stacks
And stacks
And stacks.
Kitchen table crafts,
A football by the fireplace,
Snowball has claimed the sofa.

But over here,
In this corner that's just mine
I can sit and rest my mind,
Reflect on the day's love
And not the stress.

I can choose not to see the mess.

For My Friend in Rehab

The sky brought me an angel
And I sent her on to you,
With hopes that you would know how much you're loved.

The sky brought me a rainbow
In clouds of every hue.
The storms inside your heart reflect above.

But rainbows dim and angels fly.
And you can't hear my lullaby.
It seems that these few lines will have to do.

So sleep, my sweet,
and hold on tight,
as if it were my arms embracing you.

How to Pack

When there's no room left for love,
When you have stuffed your bags so full
That the zipper moans as you close it
And the seams threaten to burst,

When the weight of obligation presses against
Your chest and the steady beat of
Shoulds and have-tos pulses in your head,

Drop everything you believe
To be essential and real.

Let them all go and feel
The breath in your lungs,
The breeze on your face,
This gentle embrace.

When there's no room for love, imagine
That love can squeeze through the narrowest of cracks,
Lay roots through a mountain of granite,
Spread across a field of doubt and insecurity,
Leaving a trail of shimmer-glazed popcorn
That will lead you back
To who you are.

When there is no room left for love, remember
That love occupies no space,
Requires no time,
Inhabits no place.

- 5 -

INDESCRIBABLE

Why is the best part,
The part I'd most like to write,
Indescribable?

Lingering

I've imagined you so often
it feels like I'm remembering
the brush of your cheek against mine
as a distant memory.
Your taste lingers in my mouth
like an aftershock of whisky.

Do you feel the softness of my flesh
against your palm when you dream?
Feel us standing together again
in that place we've never been
in form, though our souls
seem to have danced
here before?

Sometimes I Dance

Sometimes I dance in the moonlight,
Soft in my skin,
Fluid on my feet.
Limbs brush through the cool night air,
Painting new maps
In this territory between earth and sky.

Sometimes I linger in the rain,
As though its liquid would seep into my pores
To replenish me.
Languid.
The weight of the water pulls me down,
Holding me in a space
Where I can't help but remember.

Sometimes I bask in the sun,
Dressed in black and too warmly for the weather,
Absorbing as much heat as I can stand
As my left arm stretches up
And over the back of the chair.
Face tilts up.
Eyes close.
I lift my feet off the ground, extend my right leg,
And that movement sets me gently rocking.

Cradled in the perfect balance of motion and stillness,
A thought arises:
I only wanted to stop my soul from dying;
I never imagined what it would feel like
To live.

They tried to contain her

with concrete walls
and massive boulders,
sandbags piled high along the shore.
They compelled her to stay
within her bounds.

But I stood on the edge of the cliff
and watched her seep through cracks,
wash around edges,
sometimes with thunderous force,
more often with the graceful undulations
of the snakes that guard the temple in Bali,
the one that can be reached only when the tide is low.

I went there once when I was younger
and more fearful, anxious to leave
before she came back, lest I become hostage
to the rising tide and the hazards
I could not see below its surface.

Now I am not so afraid.
Now I would stay in that holy place,
enraptured by her fluid embrace,
knowing that she would show me
the path to my own liberation,

just as she would never let herself be contained.

The Hummingbird and the Fly

The heat broke, so it seemed like a good idea
to stand outside and stare into space.
Specifically, the space between the trees
above the canyon
at the level of my deck,
maybe one hundred yards out.
I'm not a good judge of distance.

I practice relaxing my eyes
(or is it my mind?)
and that cluster of trees seems to merge
into a giant amoeba-like mass, swaying and pulsing.
Shapes dissipate into holographic forms
and I begin to perceive a movement of energy
in between
where I thought there was nothing.

I look down and a hummingbird
is drinking from scarlet buds
on plants that grow below the deck.
A hummingbird!
Gray-brown with an iridescent back,
Wings flap and flap and flap as
she hovers in front of me for a moment
or two before flying off to the right.
I turn my head to follow her,

my gaze landing on a fly perched
on the neon green arm of a plastic chair.
He crawls up the length and around the side.
Maybe he is looking for water too?
Or perhaps a place to rest
before he begins the long journey across the canyon,
which to him must seem as big
as the city is to me.

I was only going to write about the hummingbird.
But then I thought,
"Why should the fly be any less remarkable?"

A Void That Contains Everything

In the deepest stillness there is movement.
In silence there is sound.

I sit in the saffron eye
of a daisy, encircled
by its deep pink, velveteen rays.
Outstretched.
Outstretching.
Open.

Bees and butterflies dance
an elaborate ballet
in, around, and through this garden.
Pollinating potential.

Their patterns of motion and rest
are as impossible to predict as
the currents of wind
that move trees to surrender
seeds of intention.

Quiet buzzes through me
until it becomes a part of me,
rearranges me
the way the vibrations of a song can change
the crystalline structure of water.

Encased in this space,
in the pregnant womb beyond time and place,
skin dissolves into ether and
I become the dancer and the dance,
the instrument and the music,
a conduit of chance.

Mystery

She
always
chooses the
mystery-flavored
lollipop, even when
her favorite, blue
raspberry, is
sitting
right
n
e
x
t
t
o
i
t.

paradox

the way we make wishes by spreading the seeds
of a weed.

the way sunlight dances on the water like rain,
shimmers like fireflies between blades of grass that grow in the lake.
the blurred edge of land and water.

the way rocks appear black and barren as they jut from the ocean
and the way flowers grow on those lifeless stones
in tones of amethyst, jade, citrine.

the way charts can predict tides, but not patterns of movement
as waves rebound off the shore
and one another.

the way salt in water can both soothe and sting.

the way my heart can hold a wellspring of grief
and also the feeling of being a bird in flight.
that it can go to the depths and still find surprise and delight
in the sweet-tart nectar of a freshly-picked peach
as it drips down my chin, the tears
as they drip down my cheeks.

the way vulnerability can be powerful,
emptiness complete,
and darkness illuminating.

and the way that I and we are one and not
the same.

Dilemma

Isn't it the dilemma of all things

that the first bite has the most flavor,
yet the taste of it makes you crave the second,

that the more intense the flavor,
the more bland everything else seems in contrast,

that the better it gets,
the better it gets,
the better it gets
in the boundless realm of possibilities,
while the density of reality begins to appear
all the more limited?

I used to drink tea from little bags
with strings attached and
clichéd quotes on the tag.
I didn't care much about brand
or type or variety.
They all seemed the same to me.

I was content, comforted even,
by the tepid brew that warmed
my mug and my belly,
until I learned of the magic to be found
in watching hand-rolled tea leaves blossom
in clear water, heated to just the right temperature;
the subtle nuances of grassy, floral, and woodsy tones;

and flavor that continued to unfold long after I set the cup down.

Immersed

It was only for a minute or two.

I was lying on the deck with my eyes closed.
Immersed
in the stillness of now,
while at the same time aware of my friend
talking on the phone only a few feet away,
of music playing on the patio speakers,
of cars shuttling back and forth on the main road.

I opened my eyes,
surprised by the sky
and the movement of the clouds above me.
Overcome
with the disoriented feeling
one might get after stepping off a roller coaster
or onto dry land after spending a month at sea,
of waking from a dream so vivid
that my mind does not remember fully
that I am of the earth
and not the sky,
and that I had been lying still the whole time.

Gratitude Is Like a Giddy Toddler

Have you ever seen something so beautiful
that you almost couldn't stand it?
Like it was a heroic effort
to contain yourself,
to refrain from jumping
up and down and shouting
like a giddy toddler
who just tasted ice cream
for the first time,
and wants to proclaim to everyone
within earshot
how magnificent it was?

The tips of the clouds at the edge
of the horizon glowed hot pink
as their condensed matter caught the light
of the setting sun below.
Billowing waves rolled toward me,
their gentle undulations punctuated
by jagged peaks
and land lakes that formed in openings
where the ground was visible
twenty thousand feet below.

The young man in the row ahead of me
angled his phone at the window
to take a picture.
And I felt relieved
that I was not the only one
who noticed.

Truth Tears

I always cry a little
when I touch
what is
real.

Possibility

Possibility came to visit me
In an early morning dream.
She was cloaked in all potential
And veiled in mystery.

I almost didn't answer
When she roused me from the deep,
Urged me to pick up the pen
'Stead of going back to sleep.

Her message was quite simple,
And I know it to be true.
So I quickly jotted down these words
To share them here with you.

While "anything is possible"
Is said time and time again,
The trick to finding rainbows is
Remembering to look for them.

ILLUSIONS

Thoughts become shackles,
Imprisoning me within
My own illusions.

The Net

"Never underestimate the importance of the net,"
he tells me on the ride to school.
Of course.
The net.

"The net has a huge impact on my shot."
That doesn't make any sense,
I think but don't say.

"Some nets are too thin," he continues.
Why would the net make a difference?
The ball doesn't touch it until after it clears the rim,
after you know whether or not the shot has gone in.

"I like a net that's a little stiff, but not too stiff."
But it just hangs there without purpose.
You can't bank the angles like you can on the backboard.
I've seen the way a funny bounce off the rim can make or break a game.
But not the net.

"Yep, it's all in the net."

Finally, I look at him and say,
"It's kinda strange."

"Yeah," he says,
"It's such a mental game."

A Poem about Spring

The birds are chattering outside my window again.

A hundred thousand shades of green paint the canyon
against a cloud-gray background.

Signs of life emerging by the minute
And I had been burrowed so deep
I didn't see the red, red, redbuds budding.
Now their branches are full flower.

Now mountain laurel's luscious purple blossoms
droop like bunches of grapes and smell as sweet.

Can I savor their fragrance before it becomes ordinary?
Before youth gives way to maturity?

I am not surprised by the first butterfly
that lands in my garden,
but I had forgotten about the bluebonnets.

It was the daisy that reminded me:
Beauty lies dormant beneath
the crusty surface of winter.

Rebel Flowers

There's a voice inside my head
That says I'm wasting time,
That I'm supposed to follow a straight line
And not spread myself out all over the place,

That I stretch too far beyond my territory,
That I'm not behaving the right way,
That I could use more discipline.

The voice was loud this morning,
But I was louder as it scolded me
About all the things I had yet to complete.
"Just stop!" I proclaimed,
"I'm taking a walk."

About a mile away from home,
I was thinking about a poem
When I was distracted
By my neighbor's yard.

Don't those flowers know
That they're supposed to grow
Straight up from the ground
And not sideways through cracks in stone walls?
Perhaps someone ought to tame them back
Before beauty becomes unruly.

The Trail Is Just a Suggestion

Hector and I met at a coffee bar.
He was working and I was ordering,
and a friendship formed
over an unusual conversation
about the color pink.

The first time Hector and I hiked together,
I blocked off what I thought
was the appropriate amount of time
for the distance we would travel,
given a moderate-to-brisk pace
and the uncertainty of having two dogs with us.

You see, I grew up in suburban Los Angeles,
in a culture where the goal of a hike
was to burn as many calories as possible
in the shortest time.

But Hector wasn't there to make good time
or cover a certain amount of ground.
He was there to explore
a new friendship,
an unfamiliar path,
the gift of a beautiful day in the woods.

An interesting leaf would catch Hector's eye,
and he would run over to investigate.
He'd stop to admire the curves
of a rotted-out tree stump.
He leaned over to feel the moss
that was forming on stones.

At one place, we reached a place that was impassable—
a tree had fallen during a heavy storm,
and there was no way around it.

"I guess we need to turn around
and go back the same way we came,"
was my obvious solution.

But Hector had a different notion.
"Or," he countered,
"we could slide down this little hill
into the creek and walk through the water
a little ways until we catch up with the trail."

I looked at the "little hill" he was referring to,
and then at Hector, and then back at the hill.

"Uh, you can slide down the hill,
but I don't think I can," I told him.

"Sure you can," he said as he held out his hand
to let me know that he would help me get down,
that I wasn't alone.

Moments later I was walking through hip-deep water,
laughing at myself
and the moment
and the great lesson that Hector had just taught me:

The trail is just a suggestion.

Falling Apart

My foundation is crumbling.
The three-inch pressed powder disc
that's enclosed in a plastic silver clamshell case,
the stuff I use to cover my face,
to smooth out the inconsistencies
while still allowing the me to shine through,
the one I waited two weeks in the mail for,
is breaking apart in chunks and falling on the floor
and into the sink where it mixes with water and forms
a muddy paste.

The zipper is busted on the neoprene sleeve
I use to protect my computer.
The grooves don't line up
so the zipper slides back and forth
and back and forth
and back and forth and back
on one track
as the fabric flips and flops,
exposing this device
on which I store my life.

My fancy Swedish SUV
will not let me into my trunk reliably.
There's a little button that operates the hydraulic elevation lift
and sometimes when I press it nothing shifts
and I have to feel around
and feel around
and feel around
in just the right way

for it to respond.
And sometimes it doesn't so I
have to fold down the rear seats
and reach through the back.

And sometimes it works with ease
and that feels like a tease.

The Landscape Is Always Changing

The landscape is always changing.
  This year the sage along the highway seems bigger,
    the snow on the mountains dwindles,
      and smoke is thick as clouds.
We are afraid of the fire.

The landscape is always changing.
  Extraordinary structures of concrete and glass,
    once so jarring,
      become part of the mundane
        as my eyes adjust to the changing scene.
Though they long for green.

This year passes with the landmarks of time,
  bringing glimpses of fading emotions
    as I let go of the story
    of a distant memory.

The landscape is always changing.
  I see it in the charred remains of the forest,
    the heat it takes to melt steel,
      the burning rage of dissidence.
And still we are afraid of the fire.

But the lodgepole pines of Yellowstone
  will only release their seeds in 150-degree heat
    and ash that falls like snowflakes
      nourishes the soil,
        readying it for new life.

Parental Controls

I tell my dad that there are times
when I'm home doing the stuff—
you know, the adulting stuff—
and I look around and think,
Where did all the grownups go
and who left me in charge?
He laughs and says that sometimes
he catches his reflection in a store window
and wonders who the old man is staring back at him?

My teenage boy's annoyed about the parental controls
on his phone which require my approval
before he can download a new app.

I tell him that sometimes parental controls are annoying
and sometimes they are helpful.
I tell him that his job is to push the boundaries
and my job is to hold them.
I don't like this part of the job very much.

Sometimes I hate that I wasted so many tired years
wanting him to grow up faster
when now all I want to do is slow things down
and keep him close a little longer.

As if I could place a parental control on time.

My little girl tells me that my New Year's resolution
should be to practice patience
because sometimes
(often)
I interrupt her questions before she finishes asking.

Because I already know what she's going to ask
and that the answer will be no.
She says she doesn't care as much about the answer.
She wants me to hear her.

I'm learning.

But I hate how often the word "No" comes out of my mouth.
Can I just have a little activity book? No.
A small Lego? No.
A make-your-own stuffed animal? No.
Pottery? No.
Froot Loops? No.
Icee? No.
Smoothie? No.
Sprite? When will you let me have Sprite? Never.
Pizza? Fine.

She and I spent so much time and excitement
looking for the perfect loft bed for her room.
I didn't stop to think how far away
she would feel as she drifts off to sleep five feet
above the ground.
And though the rule is that she sleeps in her bed on weeknights,
I smile in the morning when I wake
to see that she has landed in mine.

This boundary suddenly seems as ridiculous to me
as trying to control who my children are becoming.

"You know, she's gonna have to grow up eventually,"
her brother tells me.
I wonder if there's still a little boy inside
this wise young man who stands in front of me.
His next question: "Hey Mom,
can we make the frosting for my birthday cake?"
reassures me.

Chocolate spreads over his face
As he licks the mixer blade.
"You know," I say,
"You can use your fingers to scrape off the frosting.
You'll get more out of it that way."

Find the Joy Anyway

He said, "Your job when you leave this room
is to not deny what's happening in your life.
Whatever shit is hitting the fan at any given moment,
whatever pain or pressure you might feel, feel it.
And find the joy anyway."

There comes a moment
in every cycle class
when the room goes dark
and my heart becomes more
than the transport organ for my blood.
I become the one transported,
opening to wisdom and insight,
clarity and focus.

After the hard work is done:
the fastest sprint
the highest climb,
the tests of strength and endurance,
we ride in a strange sort of silence
created by the steady bass line
of electronic music
and a few words offered by our instructor.

Often I am alone in my own zone.
Sometimes I compose verse in my mind.
And once in a while I hear words that penetrate.
"Find the joy anyway."

Easy to say, but on days
when tears burn the backs of my eyes
it can be harder to remember
that finding joy is not a matter of searching
like a child on Easter morning
for transient treasures contained in plastic eggshells.
It's more like traveling the yellow brick road
and discovering that there are gifts in the wandering,
that there can be laughter in the moments between tears,
hope beneath fears,
a chance to shift gears and see
a little differently.
And maybe, just maybe, realize
that the joy was inside me all along.

Primal Heart

For a brief glimpse of time, she was just the right size
for me to hold in one arm.

My fingers nested her down-covered head,
the heel of my hand rested in the fold of a neck
not strong enough to support a skull still forming.
The pulse of her primal heart beat into my wrist.
I could balance her spine along the length of my forearm
while her pelvis folded into the bend of my elbow.
Without a swaddle, her legs cascaded down.
Her arms grasped the air in disjointed bursts.

Naked, she had no choice but to trust,
had not yet learned of dread
or betrayal
or loss.

No one had warned her of risk,
nor cloaked her in stories of
big bad wolves,
wicked witches,
and golden-haired girls
who steal porridge when no one is looking.

My daughter looked at me with night-black eyes
and a mouth that was convincing enough
for me to say she was smiling.
Most would have said it was just a reflex.

Her eyes released the latch of a window
in my heart that I thought I had sealed shut.
The one that introverted me within a shell
of me, myself, and I's, insulated from lows and highs,
forgetting that depths of despair have equal and opposite
peaks of joy, and that both are evidence
of my human experience.
The one that contented me with complacency
rather than testing the extent of my resiliency.

But I didn't come here to tiptoe
around the edges of being,
to rest comfortably,
halfway between fear and desire,
suffering and awe.

And neither did she.

Letting Go

I started in the garage—
easy enough to clear the space
where five-year-old paint waited
to be taken to waste recovery.

Into the closet, sorting socks
and scarves and shirts,
and finding joy in the growing pile
of items to give away.

Books challenged me
to examine where I've been
and where I'm going
and how much weight I want to carry.

I made gifts of long-lost treasures found
in forgotten crannies and nooks,
passing along stories with the tokens,
as though curating the artifacts of my life.

A stack of paper gives me pause:
If I release my attachment
to everything that has wounded me,
then who will I be?

And I think, how courageous the tree,
to let go of all its leaves and trust.

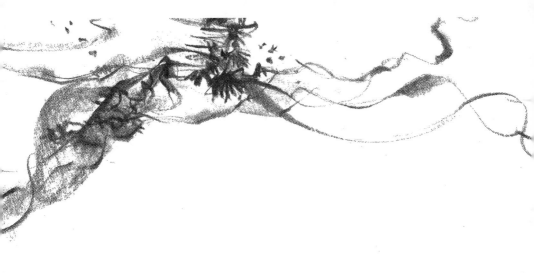

The tale began long before I was born,
Winding in strands as time spirals the **story** in all directions.
Each moment **is** but one twist in the narrative,
One glimpse which does **not** make a whole,
Imagining **who** I was in the past
Based on a self **I** see today
As I **am** rippling out into tomorrow.

Acknowledgments

Writing poetry is both a solitary endeavor and a collaborative one. This book would not exist in its current form if not for the many people who inspired, reflected on, and offered critical feedback on the writing. I would not exist in my current form if not for the relationships that nourish and challenge me. We are woven together into the fabric of the universe.

I offer a deep bow of gratitude to…

Jennifer Hritz, for editing poems and providing feedback on the overall structure of this book. We spent many sparkly hours over the past two years organizing and re-organizing, editing and re-editing. It has been a joy and a delight!

Leisl Bryant, Pamela Eakins, Martha Feferman, Melanie Greenberg, Suchi Gururaj, Laraine Lasdon, Devanshi Patel, Josep Rota, and Jen Todd, for reading drafts of this collection at various stages.

Sharon Zeugin, for inviting your creative muse to play with mine and penning the magnificent image for the cover of this book.

Levi Slayer, for your inspired graphic design work.

Phillip Estes, my poetry soulmate, for being a sounding board, a mirror, and a champion for my growth as a poet and a person.

Jeff Johnson, for our conversations in poetry that inspired many of the poems in this collection.

Hector Kriete and Andrea Loomis, for being fellow travelers on the journey of artistic expression.

Paul Matthews and Justin Jagoda, for turning my written words into songs.

Christine Arylo, James Hymes, Dan Siegel, and Ariel Spilsbury, for sharing your wisdom with me.

Angel Acosta, Sharmila Advani, Marti Ahern, Brigitte Amsberry, Robin Atwood, Gloria Bankler, Laura Berland, Diana Berrent, Wendy Betron, Vanessa Bishop, Emily Breedlove, Tyler Bryce, Paul and Ammie Busby, Nico Cary, Nichol Chase, Kasey Crown, Heidi Damata, Ann and Nigel Dawson, Mindia Gabichvadze, Maria Esther and Manuel Garcia, Robyn Goodman, Alva Greenberg, Dan Greenfield, Lea Guthrie, Stephanie Gutierrez, Karol Kaye Harris, Ryan Hill, Stacey Hoffer, Jackie Ivy, Catherine Jelinek, Michele Karron, Lindy Kummings, Leon Lasdon, Eileen Lundy, Robyn Mandelberg, Mary McCrystal, Amy Winkelstein Milstone, Selma Møller, Mamta Rathore, Gia Naranjo-Rivera, Paul Normandin, Devanshi Patel, Diego Perez, Shelly Sethi, Leslie Shaffer, Amrit Singh, Loren Stell, Kristen Skoglund, Dina Tibbs, Shelly Tygielski, Katehrine Torrini, Julia Veronesi, Adriana Vila, Andrew Villamil, Orlando, Villarraga, Amy Weidmann, Path Welch, Barnaby Willett, Justin Michael Williams, Luthern Williams, and Drew Zimmerman, for enriching my life and my writing through conversations, shared experiences, creative collaborations, and friendship.

my parents, Myrna and Steve Greenberg, for teaching me to live with an open mind, a kind heart, and a generous spirit.

my sister, Melanie Greenberg, for showing me another path that leads to where I am.

my children, for entrusting me to be your mom and for the gift of seeing the world through your eyes.

the Earth, the sky, and all the creatures who dwell upon it, for being my teachers, my guides, and a seemingly boundless source of inspiration.

everyone who is reading this book, for being a witness to my heart.

"They tried to contain her" was originally published in *di'verse'city 2019*, a publication of Austin Poets International.

"Sometimes I Dance" was originally published in *di'verse'city 2020*, a publication of Austin Poets International.

"The Path of a Butterfly" was originally published in *Pandemic Corona*, Pamela Eakins editor, 2020 (Red Earth Press).

About the Author

Jennifer Bloom is a poet, singer, scholar, and mother who believes that well-being thrives when we recognize and embrace our interconnection with all beings and the planet. She holds degrees from Yale University and the Harvard School of Public Health. She is the co-founder of Emerging Perspectives, a consulting group that uses the lenses of brain science, complexity, and reflective practice to create space for people and organizations to embrace new ways of thinking, being, and doing. Jennifer lives in Austin, Texas with her children and her dog, Snowball.

Experience more of Jennifer's poetry, music, and musings on her website, Jennifer-Bloom.com.

Find Jennifer on social media @jenniferbloom.musings.

Printed in the United States
By Bookmasters